Ten Lessons Learned

Gifts From Those Remembered

JANET MARY SINKE

To Bev
Cords

MY GRANDMA AND ME
PUBLISHERS

www.mygrandmaandme.com

Blessings
Janet Mary Sinke
2008

Acknowledgements

Special thanks to:
Natalie Pennington, whose spiritual love of all people is reflected
in the cover design and overall presentation of this special book,

my son-in-law, Mike Brya, Carmela Olivett D'Alessandro
and Linda Peckham
for their gift of time in editing,

my family, for their never ending love and support.

Sparrow Hospice Services
is part of the Sparrow Health System located in Lansing, Michigan.

Janet Mary Sinke
My Grandma and Me Publishers
P.O. Box 144
St. Johns, Michigan 48879
FAX: 989-224-3749
Website: www.mygrandmaandme.com
E-mail: info@mygrandmaandme.com

First Edition
Printed and bound in Canada
Friesens of Altona, Manitoba

Library of Congress Cataloging-In-Publication Data on File
ISBN-13: 978-0974-2732-4-2
ISBN-10: 0-9742732-4-4

Dedicated to those who have allowed me to share

in their most sacred moment:

the moment of letting go.

❧ Special Note ❧

Sparrow Hospice Services provides care throughout the entire Mid-Michigan area for the terminally ill and their families. This care is rendered by a dedicated team in the home of an indiviual or at Hospice House of Mid-Michigan.

For those who enter Hospice House the tree has significant meaning. It represents the cycle of life. Each room is identified not only with a number but with the name of a tree. It seems most fitting then, to incorporate, within the context of this book, the names and sketches of those same trees.

Elm

"May you live all the days of your life."

-Jonathan Swift-

� CONTENTS �

Hickory

*"**D**eath is not extinguishing the light;*
it is putting out the candle because
the dawn has come."

−Rabindranath Tagore−

ॐ

Dear Fellow Travelers,

There lives in every human heart, *Presence,* a *Presence* that connects us to something greater than ourselves, a Holy *Presence* breathed into every soul that enters the world, each of us a gift with purpose and meaning, born for a reason.

The stories shared here are stories of saints. No, not officially canonized saints but saints all the same, common folk, whose journey in this life has come to an end.

Their gifts of simple wisdom can light the path that will eventually lead us home.

Ten Lessons Learned,

Gifts From Those Remembered

has been eight years in the making. It is my hope that these simple yet profound stories will somehow touch your life in a positive way.

Their faces remembered. Their voices still heard.

Their memory yet thought of with sacred *Presence.*

Blessings,

Janet Mary

Walnut

"You must be part of the change you wish
to see in the world."

−Ghandi−

🐦 Beginning Thoughts 🐦

In times of great sadness when heartfelt loss fills the soul with an overwhelming sense of loneliness, it is important to remember that we are never really alone.

From our initial formation to our final surrender we are loved beyond any human comprehension by a God who is forever with us. We are, each of us, a holy temple through which the Creator works His great purpose.

With gratitude, then, for those whose purpose in this life is now complete, I pass on their gifts and share with a degree of passionate urgency this, their message;

Life is a gift and we a gift to each other.
With tender hearts and open arms,
embrace life and when in doubt

always and forevermore, choose on the side of love.

That way, when it comes our turn to leave this world,
we will be ready, and we will be remembered
as someone who made a difference.

Maple

*"The saddest of tears are shed over graves
for words left unsaid and deeds left undone."*

–Harriet Beecher Stowe–

LESSON ONE

TEARS

Let your tears come whether they stem

from joy or from sorrow.

Tears are meant to wash the soul,

to cleanse, to renew.

🍃 Reflection 🍃

We were given tears for a reason, and yet, so many times we hold tears back. More often than not, our tears spill over anyway, a release for the inner spirit to express loss and fulfillment, sorrow and joy. Let your tears come. Don't shed them alone. Instead, allow your tears to be shared and dried by someone else, for we are the hands through which others will come to know the loving comfort of the One who loves us.

Let me tell you a story:

She was 51 years old. Life had not been easy. She had endured more than her fair share of heartaches, raised a child alone, dealt with constant financial troubles and worried about a future that would now never be. She carried within her heart a quiet kind of sadness that filled far too many nights with tears shed alone. Now, her life would be cut short. Her final struggle would not take long.

She had one daughter, beautiful, age 24. They had battled over the years. Some might say it was a love-hate relationship. Both were spirited, loyal and strong in their convictions.

I liked them both. A lot. Their candid personalities, dry sense of humor and bottom line approach to problems and issues made them a likeable duo.

But as final days passed, her temperament changed. She was frustrated and withdrawn. Pain control was more of a challenge. She felt deserted and regarded herself as a burden on a daughter who now seemed distant and out of reach. Six weeks into her care and one week before she died, I found her alone in the hospital bed to which she was now confined. Alone with her tears.

Alone with her grief.

She cried for loss of independence, for nights slept alone, for a daughter she loved, for grandchildren she would never hold. She cried for her physical pain but more for her own suffering of the heart.

In another room with its door closed and drapes pulled sat her daughter, a daughter alone. Alone with tears for a lost father whose strength she now longed for. Alone with tears for brothers and sisters never born. Alone with tears for a dying mother who could no longer move without her help. She cried tears of fear, tears of anger, tears of sadness. She cried in a corner where no one could hear the sobs of a child alone and frightened.

I believe there is nothing stronger than a mother's desire to comfort her child, to hold and to soothe with a quiet voice, to reassure with a gentle hand, to love unconditionally even when life is near its end.

And so, in that moment of complete surrender, when the child within laid next to her mother and rested her head on a heart now so close to its final moment, tears were dried, the heart was uplifted and the mother smiled. Pain was gone.

Oak

"Suffering alone does not teach wisdom. To suffering must be added understanding, patience, love, openness and the willingness to remain vulnerable."

–Joseph Addison–

LESSON TWO

VULNERABILITY

To be vulnerable is to bare the soul,

to bare the soul is to reveal true colors,

to reveal true colors is to expose the beauty

of the inner self.

🍃 Reflection 🍂

When the one we love is parting and the road shared is near its end, there is at this most sacred time an unexplainable grace that fills the soul. This holy grace allows for total awareness of blessings received, quiets the inner spirit with gentle peace, and frees the heart in that most vulnerable moment, the moment of letting go.

🕊 *Let me tell you a story:*

Kevin was seven years old and "man of the house," a role he accepted quite matter-of-factly, without complaint or hesitation. He was big brother to five-year-old Matthew whom he called Mattie. Kevin's greatest concern, "Who do I call when Mom dies?"

Mom was 32. Her two boys were the love of her life. She had been a good mom, caring and devoted, her sons a reflection of her and all she had taught them.

Family members, loving and supportive, would come on a daily basis to assist at Mom's house. Her sister and brother-in-law, a caring couple, had offered many times to take Mom and her boys into their own home. It seemed like a good plan since the young couple would assume the role of parents when the end came. All arrangements had been made. Mom had insisted, though, that she and her two sons would remain a family for as long as possible in their own home until "it was time."

That time came one early spring morning, the day Mom entered Hospice House. I remember when Kevin's uncle, the soon-to-be father, sat down with me and explained his well-intended plan.

"The boys will not be coming here," he said. "They

have been through enough. They are far too vulnerable to see their mother now. She looks too sick, too frail, too weak." Kevin, he felt, needed special consideration.

"Kevin is, after all," he said, "a child. Kevin," he whispered, "would not understand."

But it was Kevin, young, innocent and vulnerable, who would show the way.

He would not be denied. He demanded to see Mom and so was brought by family. The professional team, in an attempt to prepare the young boy, frustrated him. He could not understand the purpose of their well-intended questions nor the reason for delay. His mind was clear with one thought.

Mom.

He had a gift, a picture he had drawn just for her. He was ready.

Calmly and without reservation, the seven-year-old son entered her room and went to his mother's side.

Instinctively, now close to her ear, he whispered, "I'm here." Her eyes opened.

"For you, Mom," he said.

She studied it and smiled at his innocent face.

"I love the yellow sun," her weak voice responded.

"It's beautiful, but who is this up here in the blue sky?"

He looked at her, puzzled that she needed to ask.

"It's Jesus," he said. "He's sitting in His chair. The empty chair right next to Him is for you. He's waiting for you, Mom."

She pointed to the stick figures below.

"And who are these people?"

"It's Mattie. Can't you tell? And here I am. I'm pushing Mattie high on the swing."

"Yes, I see." She took his hand, "And why are you smiling?"

He half frowned. It seemed so obvious to him.

"Because, Mom," the child continued, "you are going to a place where you won't throw up anymore. You'll sit in this chair," he pointed again, "and when you look down you will see me. You will see me right here with Mattie."

She cradled his face.

"Don't worry, Mom." He smiled. "Everything will be all right."

Spruce

"The secret to a long and fruitful life is to
forgive everybody everything
every night before you go to bed."

–Bernard Mennes Baruch–

LESSON THREE

.

FORGIVENESS

Let go of everything that prevents the spirit from
feeling whole and joyous and at peace.

🦌 Reflection 🦌

I am convinced there is nothing quite as powerful as the act of forgiveness, for through this gift the soul is allowed to feel the gentle touch of the Creator's Hand.

Don't waste a day, an hour or a moment of your life. Heal the hurt, break the silence, travel the distance to mend the fence. Experience the awesome gift of forgiveness in this moment, for there are those of us whose final opportunity to make things right lies solely with this day.

🐦 *Let me tell you a story:*

It had been a constant challenge to keep him comfortable. He was restless, couldn't sleep. His face showed expressions of sadness and agony. He had shared his family history a week before. There was no mention of any significant conflicts or problems. Two daughters at his bedside were devoted and caring. His priest had come. He had been anointed. His soul was ready. Or so it seemed. Still, he continued to struggle. Death would come hard.

Then, his request, one final request that would make all the difference.

"I want to see my son."

No one had known, only two daughters sworn to secrecy. His only son, in prison. No contact had taken place for a very long time. Now, in his final moments, his heart weighed heavy with profound sadness for years filled with silence and hurt and distance.

I don't know what caused him to make this last request. It didn't matter. We needed to act quickly for his time was short. Many doubted he would live for this final meeting to take place, but the spirit is capable of great things when longing to forgive.

Then, on a quiet, rainy afternoon, dressed in orange prison garb, wrists and ankles in shackles, he came, a young son too old for his years, his tired soul reflected in sad and darkened eyes. His weakened father, desperate for this moment, extended his frail, shaking hands then waited for his son. With slow, hesitant steps the penitent child went to the bedside, fell to his knees and silently begged forgiveness, his words expressed through quiet, heartfelt tears. A powerful moment, emotionally moving, a moment filled with untold gratitude for this precious gift of time, a father and son reunited through one loving embrace.

And the awesome power of forgiveness, given and received, freed the spirit, lifted the burden, brought peace to a tired mind and eased two weary hearts.

He died quietly two hours later.

Cottonwood

"We choose our joys and sorrows long before
we experience them."

–Kahil Gibran–

LESSON FOUR

INNER PEACE

*Inner peace is determined by choices made
and a life lived in total oneness
with the God who created us.*

🥬 Reflection 🥬

Every soul longs for inner peace: a state of contentment often determined by choices made; choices that affect not only ourselves but others as well, for our lives do not belong to us alone.

🐦 *Let me tell you a story:*

Before I began my career in hospice, I worked the midnight shift as a staff nurse in a number of medical facilities. During that time I experienced a wide variety of different people, all with unique problems and stories. Many I have forgotten.

But there is one scene from one true story that remains with me still, a Friday night I will forever remember.

I was working emergency. It was 2 a.m. when the call came, a bad accident, six teenagers involved.

I remember thinking at the time, *I have teenagers, good kids, who like any other kids, make mistakes.*

The good kids involved in this particular accident had been drinking. They were wheeled into ER rooms with dislocated shoulders, broken legs, cuts and wounds and great fear that intensified the pain of their injuries.

The dreaded calls were made. Every parent's worst nightmare. I remember wild fear on frantic faces entering through emergency room doors, their desperate need to locate their own, and their tearful prayers of gratitude upon learning all their children would live.

All, except one.

And the saddest, most heart-wrenching scene of that night took place not in occupied ER rooms, not with crying mothers and hovering fathers, not with wounded sons and daughters, but in the hallway with the Driver who had been spared any physical injury.

A big kid. A big, good kid, eighteen years old, a football player. The world and life only an hour ago had stretched out before him.

The Driver.

Head down, hands stuffed deep into jean pockets, he looked up with pleading eyes at the officer who knew the impact of the message he was about to relay.

"Your friend is dead." And with those four words the weight of the world was placed upon his shoulders.

He slumped to the floor. Shaking hands now covered his face and amidst sobs came a prayerful cry for everyone to hear, a prayer begging God to let him take it all back, a desperate cry to make it right for the burden was too great and life would never be the same.

In months and years now followed, a certain sadness remains for all those touched by that one regrettable night.

Yet, even in the darkest of hours, remorseful souls can, through faith, experience healing, the kind of healing that restores inner peace through the love of a Father who will never abandon us.

Cedar

"For I have said, 'the world was built by love.'"

−Psalms 89:3−

LESSON FIVE

AFFECTION

Embrace with both arms.

Say, "I Love You."

Hold hands.

Kiss.

Be someone with a heart not afraid

to show love.

🍂 Reflection 🍂

A newborn baby enters the world screaming for attention, a brand new spirit who quiets when held by secure, loving arms. A tiny little person calmed and made content when soothed by the sound of a mother's voice.

An amazing thing when you think about it.

And so it is all through life, each of us a mystery, each of us longing to be held, needing to be loved, each of us capable of greatness when the spirit within is nurtured with affectionate words and deeds.

🍃 *Let me tell you a story:*

It was an early spring morning when I entered the house through the back door like I had so many times before. It was still dark. An old lamp dimly lit, created a certain kind of reverent glow in the small bedroom where they both laid. I knew him well. Never did I wonder about his secret thoughts on any subject. He told it like it was and had faced his terminal disease in the same headstrong way. In his fight to maintain control of his life, his gradual loss of independence had been especially frustrating not only for him but for his entire family. He was gruff and stubborn, a man of few words. In the years I had known him, never did I witness outward signs of affection.

And yet, she loved him.

Caring and affectionate, she longed for the slightest touch. The crippling rheumatoid arthritis had left her completely bed bound for many years. Her frail condition more than once, had brought her close to her own end. For 56 years they had remained together, she, always in need of him.

But on this particular early spring morning, in a room shared together, it was he who lay dying. Every sign indicated his life was in its final moments. She watched and waited.

"Closer," she said. "I need to be closer."

And when positioned next to her husband, she tearfully relayed her heartfelt words of gratitude.

"Thank you." she said. "Thank you for loving me, for remaining at my side, for all you have been in my life."

And the man so close to his final moment, responded. He reached for her hand, took hold, and death was delayed.

For three days her affectionate words, her touch, comforted this seemingly hard-nosed old man. No pain medicine was needed as long as she lay at his side, the end moment remembered with one final squeeze of her hand, their final good-bye.

And the memory of that simple affectionate deed provided warm comfort for the few remaining months of her life. Simple affection, her warmest memory recalled with a contented smile for in the end she had held the hand of the one she loved.

Holly

*"Live how you will have wished to have lived
when you are dying."*

–Christian F. Gellert–

LESSON SIX

CELEBRATION

Put out the good dishes and crystal at dinnertime,

for there is no company more special than

your own family.

🍃 Reflection 🍃

Where would you go if you could go back in time? An interesting question when one considers the many historical events of the past.

For me, however, without hesitation, I know exactly where I would choose to go. I would go to a little farmhouse in Fowler, Michigan. I would sit at a table with my father, his fourteen brothers and sisters, my grandmother and grandfather and celebrate with them a much needed spring rain or bountiful wheat harvest.

And I would go back to a little coal mining town in Pennsylvania and celebrate Christmas with my mother. I would watch her step onto her dirt bedroom floor, put on her one good dress, and then, with family, I would walk the mile to church and celebrate Midnight Mass. Together.

I am proud of my roots, my ancestors, their sacrifices, their triumphs. I am blessed because I am part of a simple people who celebrated life.

🕊 *Let me tell you a story:*

There once was a "so-called-rich-man," rich by society's standards that is. You know, large bank account, three new vehicles in the driveway, big beautiful home. He was a chemical engineer. Brilliant. He had worked hard his whole life.

He was 40 years old, and he was dying.

And in the course of his life, his efforts, his time, his energies were dedicated mainly to the advancement of his career. There was no time to celebrate Little League wins or gold stars for second grade artwork. No time to celebrate Christmas plays or birthday parties for a seven-year-old son who now struggled to go to his father's side. There was no time to celebrate wedding anniversaries or weekends away. No time to recognize the needs of a wife who once loved him.

Now, in his final days, he took inventory of his life: career goals, accomplished; fame, achieved; and fortune filled the house where he lived with two strangers. And the choices made tipped the scale much too far to the side of material things. So the heart was empty, and the emotional connection he now longed for was not to be.

In the end the "so-called-rich-man" died alone.

Across town lived a "so-called-not-so-rich-man." You know, not so rich by society's standards, a small house, used car, waiting for payday. He was a painter by trade, worked hard, was a father of four kids, and a husband to a wife of twelve years.

He was 40 years old, and he was dying.

The "so-called-not-so-rich-man" died on a Saturday morning, and when I arrived at his home I was greeted by brothers and sisters, his mother and father, friends and neighbors, and a wife and four kids who wondered how they could possibly go on without him.

I waited with them and listened to their "remember whens." He coached Little League, fished with sons and daughters, held hands with a wife he adored. There were countless birthday celebrations, Christmas parties, new babies, baptisms, ice cream cones for eight-year-old baseball players and walks in the moonlight.

There were stories of when he was young and how he grew.

"Always a good boy," Mom would say.

And the celebrations of his life went on and on.

Take time. Make memories today. Celebrate.

Die rich like the "so-called-not-so-rich-man."

Birch

*"Humor is very powerful because it connects
you directly with your soul."*

−Author Unknown−

LESSON SEVEN

HUMOR

Never lose your ability to laugh, especially at yourself.

Be someone who is thought of and remembered

with smiles.

🌿 Reflection 🌿

Someone once said, "Laughter is the best medicine." I believe this is true even in the moment of final good-byes.

Countless times as families surround their dying loved ones, heartfelt laughter is often heard, laughter that comes from the gut, laughter that forces the lungs to expand, suck in the air and then relax the tensions of the spirit. Often, that laughter is mixed with tears and somehow the combination provides wonderful comfort, an easing of the grief, a calming for the soul. It is not unusual for family members to sometimes feel guilty at what seems to be a disrespectful response. But, to recall cherished memories that bring smiles and laughter is to give a great gift.

🐾 *Let me tell you a story:*

Harold was 83 years old. The loss of his wife had left a major void in his life. She had been his companion and soul mate for 55 years. He missed her and, "Had it not been for Gertrude, the pet collie dog," a son would later tell me, "Harold probably would have died long before now."

Gertrude would come to Hospice House to visit old Harold, and it was Harold's room where the staff was drawn. It was said that even Gertrude was caught smiling as hilarious, old stories were shared in Harold's room. The laughter, I remember, was contagious. It was the laughter that uplifted the spirits of all within hearing distance.

But as Harold grew weaker, he was confined to bed and soon became unresponsive. His five children and grandchildren kept a bedside vigil. Gertrude, now cared for by a good neighbor, no longer came to Hospice House.

Knowing Gertrude had been a special companion, a grandson came one day with a very life-like, stuffed, yellow collie dog and placed it in bed with Harold. For more than a week, the pretend animal lay at his side.

Then, the morning of his death, as I assisted with Harold's care, he moaned, opened his eyes and whispered something I couldn't quite make out. I came closer, as did his son and daughter who had stayed the night. They leaned over the bed, anxious to hear what they felt would be their father's final message.

It was quiet. We were all ears as he slightly raised a feeble finger and pointed at the fake collie. His voice, though weak, was clear.

"I think it's dead," he said.

Then one last time laughter rang from old Harold's room, a laughter mixed with tears from those who would greatly miss this light-hearted spirit, yet forever remember him with smiles and with loving laughter.

Dogwood

"To give pleasure to a single heart by a single act of kindness is better than a thousand heads bowing in prayer."

–Saddi–

LESSON EIGHT

KINDNESS

Take every opportunity to perform kind deeds,

for you may be the only candle

to light a person's darkness.

🐿 Reflection 🐿

Simple acts of kindness can change the world. Lend a shoulder for someone to rest their head, hold the hand of someone who grieves, touch the heart of someone with gentle words, perform a simple act of kindness and you are remembered for a lifetime.

🐦 *Let me tell you a story:*

It was one very special Christmas not too long ago, when I was blessed by a simple act of kindness.

Now, I must tell you, I love Christmas. I love everything about it. I love lit Christmas trees trimmed with silver and gold bulbs that glitter and sparkle from every angle. I love the hustle bustle of shoppers, the Christmas carols, the garland. I love becoming part of the whole Christmas scene.

But it is Santa's castle that I especially love where the very young wait to petition the saintly man who wears red and knows all.

Each year I inevitably find myself in front of Santa's castle. I sit and watch and go back in time, for just awhile, to another Santa and another castle where a younger mother and younger father stood with five younger sons and daughters. I like to, just for awhile, sit and remember when.

But that was a different time. Things change. We all get older.

I'm much slower now. Parkinson's does that to a body. And so on this particular Christmas shopping day, as I felt the effects of my medicine wearing thin, I knew it was time to go. So I gathered my packages and headed out.

It seemed like a long way.

And as other shoppers passed by with their normal gait and sense of balance, I felt especially slow and much older than my 52 years.

I kept looking toward the entrance where I noticed a gentleman waiting by the door. He seemed to be looking my way, but there were lots of shoppers. He could have been looking for anyone.

But as I neared the entrance, he smiled. He was waiting for me. He opened both doors as I made my way out.

Funny, how the simplest thing can make one cry.

Funny, too, how the simplest thing can become a lasting memory.

I don't know who he was. I guess it doesn't matter. But I do know this:

I will never go Christmas shopping again without thinking of that stranger. And so, from the bottom of my heart, to all strangers who take the time to smile, to notice, to hold open doors, to extend a simple act of kindness, my eternal thanks.

Chestnut

"Dance as if no one's watching;
sing as if no one's listening
and live everyday as if it were your last"

–Irish Proverb–

LESSON NINE

FUN

*I am totally convinced that a truly successful life
is measured by one's ability to say three very basic,
yet all important words,
"I HAD FUN!"*

❧ Reflection ❧

When I think back on those who have since left this world, their final days and hours spent with families and loved ones gathered, one fact remains consistently the same: memories shared at the end of life, the ones that really count, do not concern the size of a house, or how fancy the car, or how much was gained or lost in a 401K. What is remembered, talked about, enjoyed, and relived over and over again are times of all out fun.

🐦 *Let me tell you a story:*

She loved Reba McIntire. NO! I mean she REALLY, REALLY loved Reba McIntire. She was a foot stompin', official card carryin', t-shirt wearin', book totin', country music singin' Reba McIntire fan.

So naturally, when she learned of a Reba McIntire concert, there was no hesitation. She stood in line and waited long hours to purchase the precious tickets that would mark the last night of her life. At the time she had no idea of the aggressive cancer that was beginning to take hold.

Three months later, the newly diagnosed disease had spread quickly. She had lost weight, was weak and now confined to a hospital bed. Her loss of independence, however, did not defeat her fun-loving spirit. Why even her once bald head, a side effect from intense chemotherapy, became a source of excitement as blonde fuzz sprouted just in time for the concert.

The big night came, and she was still with us. There had been doubt as to whether she would live long enough for this much anticipated event. I, too, had worried, but upon arriving at her home I found her dressed and ready to go. She sported a new print pair of slacks and matching blouse. Her nails were freshly manicured. There was a western hat and a vest with beads and tassels.

Once safely transferred into the ambulance, her daughter, hospice volunteer, nurse aide and myself, together with the driver and his assistant, all crowded in and the fun began. A sign on the vehicle's outside door announced our destination, "Reba, Here We Come."

And as we made our way, the cork to the champagne bottle was popped, glasses filled, the taste savored. We toasted one another. We toasted those we loved. We toasted those we didn't love. We toasted the President. We toasted the Queen of England and all those who passed with honking horns and thumbs up. We laughed at our own ridiculous jokes, and we toasted some more.

Upon arrival, she was carefully taken to her viewing spot. She was greeted by strangers, shook hands, said thanks and offered a warm smile that never left her face. She laid on her stretcher for three hours, proud of her new blonde fuzz, clapping to the rhythm while singing each song (for she knew them all by heart). And as I watched, I marveled at her spirit.

She couldn't walk, couldn't sit, couldn't dance.
Didn't matter.

She was dying. She didn't care.

She was here. She was in the moment, and she would have the time of her life.

She died eight hours later in the early morning.

That was ten years ago. That memory has not faded, for every time I hear a Reba McIntire song I think of her and smile because on one very special evening, one very special memory was made, a memory filled with fun.

Willow

"Make memories today that you may have roses in December."

-Sir James Matthew Barrie-

LESSON TEN

REMEMBRANCE

Someone once said,

"You're not dead until you're forgotten."

I will remember certain smiles, gentle voices,

open arms and caring eyes.

I will remember you.

➷ Reflection ✿

We may never become a world leader or high church official. Chances are slim that you or I will be the one to discover a life-saving serum for cancer or AIDS. Most of us will never step foot outside a space station to see the world and the heavens from what must be a breathtaking viewpoint.

Yet, we are a miracle, born with purpose and meaning, part of a master plan and remembered for our own unique gifts.

🐦 *Let me tell you a story:*

She was only 31 years old. She was a daughter, a sister, a wife to a loving husband and the mother of a three year old little girl named Jessica. I grew to know and to love this young woman in the eight weeks I cared for her. At each visit she would take my hand, and I would listen to her "remember whens," stories of her past filled with simple memories recalled in all-too-short a life. Her told recollections and the images etched in my mind from those eight weeks are now part of my own stored memories.

I will remember her devoted mother-in-law and father-in-law, their unconditional love reflected in day-to-day attentive care.

I will remember her only sister's new born baby daughter and the reverence with which this small child was placed into frail, extended arms, a niece, whose name would come to symbolize the memory of a sister and the renewal of life itself.

I will remember her only brother, his silent pain felt in their final good–bye.

I will remember her father, a big man with strong protective arms that gently held and rocked a dying daughter, his soft kiss to her hair, his quiet escape to the outside January cold, his broken heart unaware of falling snow that now melted on cheeks made warm with tears.

I will remember a little girl with curly red hair in pigtails cuddled next to her mother, unaware of the inevitable parting that would soon take place.

I will remember her young husband, the way he held her hand, the way he touched her face. His total devotion.

I will remember her courage, her love of family, her final acceptance in the end.

I will remember.

"*We are each of us angels with only one wing;
and we can fly only by embracing one another*"

–Luciano DeCrecenoa–

🐝 Angels Among Us 🐝

There are those angels in this world who are called to a special vocation, angels who become part of life's sacred mystery, angels who are remembered for a lifetime.

Sparrow Hospice Services is blessed to have many such angels. Through their commitment and gift of self, thousands have experienced a death with dignity. The untold gratitude felt toward these angels of hospice cannot be measured.

As I think back on my own experiences, I am especially grateful to those intial angels who laid the groundwork, established standards of excellence, and worked tirelessly to promote a program so vital to the community. To those first angels who still remain and continue to serve others through hospice, I extend my own heartfelt appreciation for the distinct honor of working with you. Your names are forever embedded in my memory.

I know an angel. Her name is Carol. She was the first physician to act as Medical Director of Hospice. Her caring hands and gentle spirit continue to teach others through example, the true meaning of compassionate care.

I know an angel. Her name is Michelle. Through her leadership and dedicated effort, all terminally ill members of the community are offered the option of hospice care, be they rich or poor, well-to-do or homeless, friend or stranger; Michelle, my mentor and friend for many years.

I know four very special angels. Their names are Sue, Kay, Gwen and Karen. They are the nurses whose leadership skills and compassionate hearts open the door to hospice and reassure those who face a terminal disease that they are not alone.

I know several other very special angels. They are Meredith, Pearl, Karen, Laurie, Sybil, Patsy, Lyn, Dawn, Lanye, Merna, Susan and Pam. These are the nurses who take under their wings the overall needs of the dying. They provide and maintain comfort by alleviating physical pain. They hold the hands of those who grieve. They are true healers of the spirit.

There are three angels named Karen, Julie and Angie. These are the nursing assistants whose hands bathe, dress, comfort, and feed. They render care with genuine smiles and holy reverence.

There are three very special angels who serve as

social workers, Mary, Jeannie and Barb. They listen with quiet wisdom. They speak to the needs of the heart. They address the unique concerns of each individual and help surviving loved ones find meaning and purpose in their lives once again.

I have come to know many angels who provide spiritual support. They are patient and loving, and always willing to address the diverse religious beliefs and rituals of those who enter hospice.

There are many angels known as hospice volunteers. Their caring hearts, unique talents and countless hours of service are invaluable in meeting the needs of the dying.

There are three other angels named Rose, Sharon and Delores, the clerical staff, who work quietly behind the scenes, day-in and day-out. Their endless list of duties, patiently tended to, has allowed the hospice program to grow and expand throughout the community it serves.

May all the caring angels of hospice who serve those entrusted to their care be blessed as they carry on with their important work. Then, through their example and the example of good people everywhere, may we all come to realize that angels are indeed among us.

Magnolia

"Remember,
the wood is made more beautiful
when branches of all kinds intertwine
and reach for the sun's rays together."

–Janet Mary Sinke–

🐦 Final Thoughts 🐦

As mortal travelers on a journey, we are placed on a road marked with change, different directions leading to alternate paths. Some paths we choose, others are beyond our control. But each path, whether chosen or not, allows us to travel only in the present, one moment at a time, all our days numbered. With countless others, we travel together, each of us with purpose and meaning, each of us a manifestation of divine grace.

We are God's *Tears* and His Hand that wipes them dry. We are His *Inner Peace* passed on to those who are searching and *Vulnerable*. We are the angels through which His *Forgiveness*, His *Kindness*, His *Affection* is made known. We are His *Humor*, His reason to *Celebrate*, to have *Fun*, to enjoy. We are the very face of God Himself, a reflection of His constant and abiding Love, the reason for our own *Remembrance*.

Walk with renewed step down the path of your life, ever mindful of God's Presence. Be open to His mystery and to new ways of understanding. Delight in the wonder of those whose paths intertwine with your own for they can take you to new and different heights where the view is spectacular and where discovery and surprise make for an exciting and holy adventure.

🐦 Hospice Note 🐦

Hospice care is a very special kind of care, a gift, lovingly provided to those who have come to the final stage of their life. Great care is taken to assure that a patient die with dignity and that those who survive are comforted by a positive experience before, during and after a loved one's death.

For those facing a terminal illness, know you are not alone. The National Hospice and Palliative Care Organization and your local Hospice care provider can help you make a well informed decision and guide you down a path that can truly hold some of the most beautiful moments of your life.

National Hospice and Palliative Care Organization
(NHPCO)
1700 Diagonal Road, Suite 625
Alexandria, Virginia 22314
703/837/1500 (phone)
703/837/1233 (fax)
Website: www.nhpco.org
E-mail: info@nhpco.org

Other books written by Award-Winning Author
Janet Mary Sinke.
(Grandma Janet Mary®)

A series of children's books meant to promote love,
honor, respect; each generation for the other.

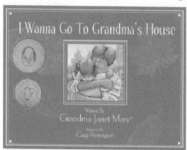

Books available online or through gift stores and major
book retailers.

Website: www.mygrandmaandme.com
E-mail: info@mygrandmaandme.com